LAKE F
RO

D1243718

W

EXTREME SURVIVAL IN THE MILITARY

SURVIVAL IN THE WILDERNESS

EXTREME SURVIVAL IN THE MILITARY

EXTREME SURVIVAL
IN THE MILITARY

SURVIVAL
IN THE WILDERNESS

CHRIS McNAB

**Introduction by Colonel John T. Carney. Jr., USAF-Ret.
President, Special Operations Warrior Foundation**

MASON CREST

Mason Crest
450 Parkway Drive, Suite D
Broomall, PA 19008
www.masoncrest.com

Printed and bound in the United States of America.

10 9 8 7 6 5 4 3 2 1

Series ISBN: 978-1-4222-3081-7
ISBN: 978-1-4222-3087-9
ebook ISBN: 978-1-4222-8779-8

Cataloging-in-Publication Data on file with the Library of Congress.

Picture Credits
Australian Army: 13, 56; **Corbis:** 6, 47, 49, 50; **TRH:** 8, 20, 23, 32, 38, 40, 44.
Illustrations courtesy of; Amber Books, De Agostini UK and the following supplied by Patrick Mulrey: 16.

ACKNOWLEDGMENT
For authenticating this book, the Publishers would like to thank the Public Affairs Offices of the U.S. Special Operations Command, MacDill AFB, FL.; Army Special Operations Command, Fort Bragg, N.C.; Navy Special Warfare Command, Coronado, CA.; and the Air Force Special Operations Command, Hurlbert Field, FL.

IMPORTANT NOTICE
The survival techniques and information described in this publication are for educational use only. The publisher is not responsible for any direct, indirect, incidental or consequential damages as a result of the uses or misuses of the techniques and information within.

DEDICATION
This book is dedicated to those who perished in the terrorist attacks of September 11, 2001, and to the Special Forces soldiers who continually serve to defend freedom.

CONTENTS

KEY ICONS TO LOOK FOR:

Text-Dependent Questions: These questions send the reader back to the text for more careful attention to the evidence presented there.

Words to Understand: These words with their easy-to-understand definitions will increase the reader's understanding of the text, while building vocabulary skills.

Series Glossary of Key Terms: This back-of-the book glossary contains terminology used throughout this series. Words found here increase the reader's ability to read and comprehend higher-level books and articles in this field.

Research Projects: Readers are pointed toward areas of further inquiry connected to each chapter. Suggestions are provided for projects that encourage deeper research and analysis.

Sidebars: This boxed material within the main text allows readers to build knowledge, gain insights, explore possibilities, and broaden their perspectives by weaving together additional information to provide realistic and holistic perspectives.

INTRODUCTION

Elite forces are the tip of Freedom's spear. These small, special units are universally the first to engage, whether on reconnaissance missions into denied territory for larger, conventional forces or in direct action, surgical operations, preemptive strikes, retaliatory action, and hostage rescues. They lead the way in today's war on terrorism, the war on drugs, the war on transnational unrest, and in humanitarian operations as well as nation building. When large scale warfare erupts, they offer theater commanders a wide variety of unique, unconventional options.

Most such units are regionally oriented, acclimated to the culture and conversant in the languages of the areas where they operate. Since they deploy to those areas regularly, often for combined training exercises with indigenous forces, these elite units also serve as peacetime "global scouts" and "diplomacy multipliers," a beacon of hope for the democratic aspirations of oppressed peoples all over the globe.

Elite forces are truly "quiet professionals": their actions speak louder than words. They are self-motivated, self-confident, versatile, seasoned, mature individuals who rely on teamwork more than daring-do. Unfortunately, theirs is dangerous work. Since 'Desert One"—the 1980 attempt to rescue hostages from the U.S. embassy in Tehran, for instance—American special operations forces have suffered casualties in real world operations at close to fifteen times the rate of U.S. conventional forces. By the very nature of the challenges which face special operations forces, training for these elite units has proven even more hazardous.

Thus it's with special pride that I join you in saluting the brave men and women who volunteer to serve in and support these magnificent units and who face such difficult challenges ahead.

Colonel John T. Carney, Jr., USAF-Ret.
President, Special Operations Warrior Foundation

An elite soldier takes part in a wilderness survival course. Given very little provisions, he must fend for himself in extreme conditions.

WORDS TO UNDERSTAND

improvise: Make something using whatever is handy.

operation: A military activity.

thermal: Material that's designed to keep heat from leaving your body.

dehydrated: Dried; all water removed.

WHAT TO WEAR & CARRY

The soldiers of the Special Forces need clothing that will withstand hostile weather and terrain. Good equipment is also vital. A few key items can mean the difference between life and death. This chapter explains the principles they teach for selecting clothing and gear for backpacking in wild areas. All travelers should carry the right equipment to help them overcome any disasters that they may face.

If you have just survived a plane crash or similar accident, the chances are that you will be dressed in light, comfortable clothes that are totally unsuitable for survival situations. This being the case, you must **improvise**. However, if you are a backpacker or adventurer, you should be better clothed and equipped to deal with a survival situation. There is really no excuse for wearing inappropriate clothing and carrying poor equipment. Today, there is an amazing variety of clothing available to the backpacker. Above all, you must select the proper clothing for the job.

But how do you know how to equip yourself? Simple: read this book, go through magazines dedicated to outdoor pursuits, go to camping exhibitions, go to camping and survival stores, and talk to the staff who have a knowledge about such things. In short, like members of the Special Forces, find out about

A thick, waterproof jacket, insulating hat, and stout walking boots are an essential part of any wilderness survival kit.

your **operation** before you set out. By doing this, you will not find out the hard way that your clothing is totally unsuitable for the wilderness.

Gore-Tex® is an excellent material for outdoor clothing. It is a "breathable" material. This means that it lets tiny drops of sweat exit but prevents water from entering. Such amazing material is not cheap, but what price do you put on your life? Of course, just wearing a Gore-Tex® jacket is not enough. In the wilderness, the weather can go from bright, hot sunshine to freezing winds in a matter of hours, particularly if you are on a remote hillside or deep in an isolated woodland. That is why you should follow what the world's Special Forces and survival experts call "the layer principle."

The layer principle is very simple. The more layers of clothing you wear, the warmer you will be. Temperature control is very easy. If you are too hot, take off clothes; if you are too cold, put on clothes. Remember, getting too hot can be as much of a problem as being too cold. If you sweat when it is cold, the body chills when you stop sweating, and your sweat-soaked clothing will draw away body heat into the air. It is important that you prevent this. Here are the layers you should wear:

- Next to the skin, you should wear **thermal** clothing (long underwear).
- Over this, wear a woolen or wool mixture shirt.
- On top of this, wear a woolen or good fiber-pile sweater, jacket, or fleece.
- As a final layer, choose a warm windproof and waterproof jacket. This should be made out of Gore-Tex® or a similar material.

Footwear

Footwear is incredibly important to soldiers in the special forces. For any outdoor activity, it is best to equip yourself with a pair of strong, waterproof boots high enough to support your ankles, never running shoes. It is important o look after your boots, and it is always wise to carry a spare pair of laces around with you.

Keep the boots supple and waterproof with a coating of wax or polish. Always check your boots before you use them for broken seals, worn-out treads, cracked leather, rotten stitching, and broken fastening hooks. There is no reason why you will not be able to get up to 10 years of use out of your boots if you take care of them. Many soldiers protect their boots further by wearing nylon gaiters over them to help keep water out when walking through wet grass and snow.

Socks are another important item of footwear. Most backpackers wear two pairs of socks on their feet for comfort and to prevent blisters. Whether you wear a thin pair and a thick pair, two thin pairs, or two thick pairs, is up to you. Find a combination you are happy with.

Pants

In terms of pants, you should have two pairs. The inner pair should be windproof, and the outer pair should be waterproof. The waterproof pair fit over your pants and should have a side zipper to let them be put on if you are wearing a pair of boots.

Jacket

Your jacket must be both windproof and waterproof. It should have a large hood (you can wear a hat underneath it) that protects all of your head, including the chin. The sleeves should have wrist fasteners to stop your body heat escaping, and it should be long enough to cover the tops of the thighs. It should also draw tight at the bottom and around the waist. Remember to choose a big one—you will have to wear lots of other clothing underneath it if the weather turns cold.

MAKE CONNECTIONS: CARING FOR YOUR BOOTS

When they have to march on foot, often over long distances, soldiers have good rules for the care of their boots.

- Stuff wet boots with newspaper and dry them in a warm, airy place. Do not dry them over a fire. This will bake and then crack the leather.
- Your boots should be of a size that lets you wear two or three pairs of socks underneath.
- Socks that are too tight will restrict the blood flowing to your feet. This can lead to frozen feet.
- Always carry a spare pair of socks.
- Whenever feet get wet, change socks as quickly as possible.

Gloves and hat

Finally, complete your clothing with a good pair of gloves and a hat. Both should be made of thermal material. The hat is especially important, as much of your body heat is lost through your head in cold weather. Pick something that covers your scalp, ears, forehead, and the back of your neck. One that stands up from the top of your head can be good as the space traps warm air.

All of this clothing is designed to protect you if the weather drops cold. This tends to be the most serious in wilderness settings. If weather gets hot, then there is usually plenty of shelter, and water is often easy to find in woodland, mountainous, or hilly regions. Also, you can take clothes off if you are too

Australian uniforms reflect the terrain of the Australian wilderness. This soldier's gun has a blank firing device fitted on the muzzle.

warm, but you cannot put them on if you do not have them. Adopt the same procedures as the special forces—prepare for anything.

Equipment & Gear

Armies have a simple rule: do not carry useless weight. No one would consider carrying bricks and other useless weight in their backpack. However, if you have a tent, for example, that is totally unsuitable for the terrain you are in, you're carrying around dead weight. Why carry around bulky cans of food when you can have lightweight packets of nutritious **dehydrated** food? You should carry only those things that help you to survive.

The survival tin can be one of your most useful pieces of equipment. If you're equipped with the items listed below, your chances of survival are much better, whatever the terrain or weather conditions. These items of equipment are not expensive or complicated. They can be fitted into any small tin. Ge used to carrying the tin around with you at all times. (It can easily fit into mos jacket pockets.) Pack the contents with cotton wool—it insulates the content and stops it rattling and, because cotton wool is flammable, it can also be usec for making fire.

Your survival tin should include the following items:

- Matches. Use these only when other fire-making methods fail.
- Candle. This will give you a source of light and help you to start a fire Candle wax can be also be eaten in an emergency.
- Flint. Make sure you have a flint with a saw striker. These can be usec to make hundreds of fires, and will carry on working long after you matches have been used up.
- Sewing kit. This is useful for repairing clothes.
- Water purification tablets. These will help you have clean water to drink
- Compass. A small button, liquid-filled compass is the best, but check i regularly for leaks.
- Mirrors. As they are reflective, they can be used for signaling.
- Safety pins. These are useful for securing items of clothing and fo making fishing lines.
- Fish hooks and line. The fishing kit should also include split lead weights Have as much line as possible—it can also be used to catch birds.
- Wire saw. This can cut even large trees (cover it in a film of grease to protect it against rust).
- Large plastic bag. This can be used to carry water and used as the linin; for a solar still to make water (The next chapter will tell you how to mak a solar still.).

- Snare wire. A brass wire is the best that can be used for animal traps.

Tents and shelters

If you are sleeping outdoors, you will obviously need a tent. There is a vast range of tents from which to choose. Most modern tents are not heavy, so go for a tent that has plenty of space inside. Bivi-bags are another type of portable shelter. In reality, they are a waterproof overall for a sleeping bag. Some have hoops that make them into one-person tunnel tents. It is not really practical to cook inside a bivi-bag, because it is so confined, but it is windproof, waterproof, and very lightweight.

Cooking

The right cooking equipment is also important. There are lots of cooking stoves to choose from, but there are two very important rules you should bear in mind when making your choice:

Keep it as lightweight as possible.

Do not buy a stove that has a lot of delicate pieces—they can be easily snapped off and lost when being used in the outdoors.

You will need cookware and crockery to go with your stove and there is a large variety available. They usually come in sets of four or five items that fit inside one another to form a very compact set—excellent for space-saving. However, before you rush out and buy a set, ask yourself if you really need this amount of cooking pans. For crockery, you obviously want a set that is hard-wearing and light. Plastic is probably the best; it is tough and will not rust.

Food

So what food should you take with you into the wilderness? The backpacker should carry dehydrated food that is made for outdoor pursuits. This means that it will contain all the right ingredients to give you energy and keep you healthy. As a general rule, avoid cans: they are bulky and awkward to carry. There are many camping foods available that come in sealed packets. All you do is pour in hot water and stir, then wait for a couple of minutes, and you have a hot, nutritious meal. In addition, there are many survival ration packs that you can purchase. These tend to be compact packs that contain meals and can keep you going for 24 hours. Here is an example of the contents of a 24-hour ration pack issued to a soldier

- Breakfast—warm oatmeal, drinking chocolate.

- Snack—chicken spread, cookies (fruit and plain), chocolate, chocolate caramels, nuts and raisins, dextrose sweets.

- Main meal—vegetable soup, curried beef granules, rice, peas, apple, and apricot flakes.

The contents of a survival tin, including flint and striker, sewing kit, candle, matches, compass, fishing equipment, and painkillers.

Backpacks

Everything you take with you needs to be carried, so you will need a backpack

MAKE CONNECTIONS: SURVIVAL KNIVES

A knife is extremely important in a survival situation. It can be used for many things, such as skinning animals, preparing fruits and vegetables, and cutting trees. Always keep your knife clean and sharp and make sure it is securely fastened when you are traveling. There are many knives to choose from, but it is best to have one that has a single blade and a wooden handle. Never throw your knife into trees or into the ground because you could damage it or it could become lost.

There are many backpacks available to the adventurer, large and small. However, remember to get a pack that is suited to your needs. If you get a 26-gallon (100-liter) pack when really you need only a 13-gallon (50-liter) one, you will probably end up filling the large pack to the brim and carry around too much weight.

Find a backpack that is comfortable and easy to use. Here are some of the things you should look for when buying a backpack:

• Side pockets, useful for carrying items that you need to get to quickly.
• Base compartment, a good place for putting wet items so they do not soak the rest of your equipment.
• Double stitching to increase strength and protection.

TEXT-DEPENDENT QUESTIONS

1. Explain the layering principal.
2. Why do backpackers wear two pairs of socks?
3. Describe the items of clothing necessary when backpacking.
4. List the items in a good survival kit.
5. What are the three steps for making a horseshoe pack?

Making a pack

There is also the horseshoe pack that can be used to carry items over long distances. Here's how to make one: lay a square-shaped material five feet by five feet (1.5 m x 1.5 m) on the ground (see the previous page: A). Place all items on one side of the material and then roll the material with the items to the opposite edge. Tie each end and have at least two evenly spaced ties around the roll (B). Then bring both ends together and secure. What you now have is a compact and comfortable pack, which you can change from shoulder to shoulder if required (C).

Sleeping bag

Finally, one essential piece of survival kit is the sleeping bag. Good sleeping bags are filled with "down," the best insulating material. In wet conditions, you will need a waterproof cover for a down-filled bag. If you know you will be sleeping in wet conditions, then you should get a bag filled with PolarGuard®.

RESEARCH PROJECT

Go online and see what dehydrated foods are available. Then go to the U.S. government's MyPlate website (ChooseMyPlate.gov), which will give you the amounts of each food group you need to build healthy meals. Using MyPlate, pick the dehydrated foods you would need for a weekend backpacking track. Make sure to include each food group, using the proportions MyPlate gives. List the menus for each meal. Then write down the cost for these foods, if you were to buy them, and add them. How much will the food cost for your weekend trip? What if you know you will be going on five backpacking trips this year, and so you buy dehydrated foods in bulk? How much money would you save per trip?

You could opt for an all-weather sleeping bag that is light but expensive. They consist of a sleeping bag, a fleece liner, and a bivi-bag.

If you are carrying all these items, then you do not really have to worry about survival. However, disaster can strike and the special forces soldier needs to know how to find food and water if he or she runs out of supplies.

WORDS TO UNDERSTAND

temperate: Not too hot, and not too cold.

lethargy: A lack of energy.

WATER & FOOD

Of all the elements of survival, water is the most important. Without water, there is no life. Therefore all soldiers must know where to find, and how to prepare, water if they are to live in the wild for any length of time. No matter where you are, there are also many types of plant and animal foods available. Soldiers must learn where to find them, how to recognize them, how to collect or trap them, and be able to tell what is poisonous and dangerous.

In a survival situation, a person may be able to live without food for weeks in certain conditions. Without water, however, he or she will die within days. Therefore, finding water is the number-one priority for all survivors. In a **temperate** climate, a person needs to drink at least a half gallon (2.5 liters) of water a day. Even if you are doing very little physical activity, you need water to replace fluids lost. Dehydration—when you lose more water than you are drinking—is a life-threatening condition. The symptoms are a loss of appetite, **lethargy**, impatience, sleepiness, stress, slurred speech, and a failure to think straight. The treatment is straightforward: replace lost fluids by drinking water.

Because sweating and breathing too hard can make dehydration worse if the survivor does not have plenty of water, you should do the following:

- Keep all physical activity to a minimum.
- Perform all tasks slowly to save energy, and take regular rest periods.
- In hot climates, work at night or during the cooler parts of the day.

To make a flask of clean and safe water, this soldier is pouring it into his Pre-Mac PWP personal water purifier.

- Keep clothing on to reduce fluid loss. There is a temptation to take off clothing in hot climates. Don't!
- Wear light-colored clothing in hot weather: it reflects the sun's rays and keeps you cooler.

Water bottles should be an essential item in any backpacker's kit. Plastic and aluminum models are available, though remember aluminum ones can be placed in a fire to heat the water if required.

If you do not have plenty of water with you, you will have to find natural sources of water. Luckily, wooded, hilly, or mountainous areas usually have many streams, freshwater lakes, or other water sources. The following signs are often an indication that water is close by:

- Swarming insects. Look out especially for bees and columns of ants.
- Birds. These may gather around water.
- Lots of plants of many different types. This often means that the plants are drinking from water that is near the surface.
- Animals. At dusk and dawn, many animals, especially those that eat grass, need water.
- Large clumps of lush grass.
- Springs and water seeping in rocky terrain.
- Cracks in rocks with bird dung outside. This may indicate a very small or narrow water source that can be reached by a straw.
- Valley floors. Dig along their sloping sides to find water.

Solar still

If you can't find water, there are several ways of collecting it. A solar still is one of the best. Dig a hole three feet (90 cm) across and two feet (60 cm) deep. Dig a small hole in the middle of the bigger hole and put a container in it. Then place a plastic sheet over the hole and hold it in place around the edges with sand, dirt, or rocks. Place a rock in the center of the sheet. When it gets hot, water vapor condenses on the underside of the plastic sheet and runs down into the container.

Transpiration bag

If you are in a wooded area, a transpiration bag is a very simple way of getting water. Place a large plastic bag over the living limb of a tree or large shrub. The bag opening is sealed at the branch. The limb is then tied or weighted down so that water will flow to the corner of the bag. Of course, an even better way of getting water is by catching rain water. A simple method of collecting rain water is to wrap a cloth around a slanted tree and ensure the bottom of the cloth drips into a container.

Webbing" is the term used for the system of belts, straps, and pouches a soldier uses to hold his kit. The pouches here contain ammunition, a water bottle, and rations.

MAKE CONNECTIONS: IDENTIFYING CONTAMINATED WATER

As well as purifying any water they find, elite forces soldiers are trained to identify poisonous water sources and avoid them. Look for the following signs that water is not healthy to drink:

- It smells bad.
- It has foam or bubbles on the surface.
- It has a strange color.
- It has no healthy plants growing around it.

Purifying water

When you have taken water from a stream or river, you will need to both filter it and purify it before you drink. Remember, filtering does not purify water, it only removes the solid particles like bits of soil. One way to filter the water is to pour it through a piece of cloth such as a cotton T-shirt. Do this a few times if possible. Then you have to purify it. This means that you kill any diseases or nasty infections that might lurk in the water. Soldiers are taught these three simple ways of purifying water:

- Use water purification tablets. (Use one tablet if the water is clear water, two if it is cloudy.)
- Five drops of 2 percent iodine in a container of clear water; 10 drops in cloudy or cold water. (Let it stand 30 minutes before drinking.)
- Boil water for 10 minutes.

If you follow these procedures, then you should have plenty of water to keep you alive in the wilderness. If you are struggling to find water, however, reduce the amount you eat. The process of digesting food uses a lot of your body's water. If you cannot find any water at all, it is best not to eat anything until you find a proper water source.

Food & Cooking

Elite soldiers are taught many different types of cooking for the wild. Food can be boiled in a metal container, or in coconut shells, sea shells, turtle shells, and half sections of bamboo. Food can also be fried by putting a flat piece of rock on a fire; when it is hot, fry food on it. Baking takes a bit more hard work. Make an oven by digging a pit under a fire. Another method of baking is to line a pit with dry stones and build a fire in the pit. As the fire burns down, scrape the coals back and put your food container in. Then cover it with a layer of coals and a thin layer of dirt. The food will then bake. Roasting is easier, as it can be done with a skewer or spit over an open fire.

Plant food

So what food can you actually eat? Let's look at plants first. There are thousands of edible plants in the wild. The survivor should carefully examine the area he or she is in for edible plant species.

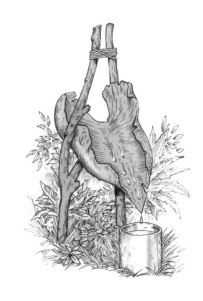

This improvised water catcher uses a leaf as a gutter. The rainwater is directed down the leaf and into a metal container beneath it.

If you have to eat unknown plants, you must carry out the taste test to see if they are safe to eat (see page 30). It is important to test all parts of the plant—many plants have only one or more edible parts.

It is impossible here to list all the edible plants you will find in the wild. Use these simple army guidelines, used by many forces around the world (including the U.S. Special Forces), to guide you as to whether something is safe or not.

- Umbrella-shaped flowers are generally poisonous. However, carrots, celery, and parsley are the exceptions to this rule.
- Beans and peas can make you feel sick and give you stomach ache or diarrhea.
- Avoid all bulbs.
- All white and yellow berries are poisonous; half of all red berries are also poisonous.
- Blue or black berries are generally safe to eat.
- Single fruits on a stem are usually edible.
- A milky sap means that the plant is usually poisonous.
- Plants that make your skin itch when you touch them should not be eaten.
- Plants that grow in water are generally edible and often tasty.

Animal food

Plants are only one source of food. Animals are another. You must become good at hunting and trapping to use animals as a food source to survive. Learn about the types of animals that live in the area you are in, their tracks, habits, and where they sleep. All animals will provide you with meat of one kind or another. However, unless you have a gun, you will catch most animals with snares and traps. Most of what you will catch in this way will be small animals and birds.

If you do have a gun, bow and arrow, or spear, obey the following rules when hunting prey: Walk as quietly as possible. Move slowly and stop frequently to listen. Be observant. Blend in with the terrain features if you can. Be prepared; animals often startle the hunter and catch him off guard.

Mammals are probably the best food source for the survivor. They are divided into the following groups:

Wild cats. These vary in size from small domestic cats to lions and tigers. Depending on the size of cat, you will either need a spring snare or a gun.

Wild dogs. Although they can be caught with snares, wild dogs are best avoided because they have a nasty bite.

Bears. They should only be tackled if you have a gun. They are large and strong creatures which can kill a person easily, so beware.

Weasels, stoats, mink, martens, and polecats. All these animals have sharp teeth and can give a nasty bite.

Wolverines—badger-shaped animals. These should be tackled only if you have a gun.

Badgers. These are an excellent food source that can be caught in spring snares and deadfall traps.

Cattle. Large cattle, especially bulls, can be dangerous.

Deer and antelope. The small types can be caught in snares and deadfalls, and the larger ones by spear traps and larger deadfalls. But beware of their horns, as they can gorge and stab and inflict serious wounds.

- Wild pigs. Their tusks can cause serious injury. They can be caught with strong spring snares, deadfalls, and pig spear traps.
- Rodents and rabbits are plentiful and easily caught with snares.
- Reptiles. They can be a valuable food source, but some can be extremely dangerous. Reptiles that are best left alone: crocodiles, alligators, Gila monsters, and beaded lizards. Do not eat toads because they have toxic skin secretions.
- Snakes. Treat all snakes as dangerous and poisonous, even if they are not. Use a forked stick to pin them down just behind the head. Then club the back of the head with another stick. Better still, cut off the head with a machete. Never pick up a snake until you are sure it is dead.
- Snails, worms, and slugs. Eat these only when they are fresh. Avoid snails with brightly colored shells because they are poisonous. Avoid sea snails in tropical waters, as some have stings that can kill. With worms, starve them for a day or squeeze them between the fingers to clear out their insides.

Snares and traps

Of course, all these animals need to be caught before you can eat them. The main type of traps are snares, deadfall traps, and spear traps. A snare is a wire or string loop placed in such a way that an animal is forced to put its head through it.

The snare will then tighten, thus killing the animal (though sometimes not immediately). Deadfall traps are simple: when the bait is taken by the animal, a weight falls on the prey and kills it. There are many types of deadfall triggers—the bit of the traps that causes the weight to fall. Most are activated by a tripwire or when the animal knocks away a stick that is holding up the weight. Spear traps can be very effective. These are a springy shaft that is held in place by a tripline.

MAKE CONNECTIONS: TASTE TEST

Use this simple test for establishing whether a plant is safe to eat. It cannot be applied to fungi—many are deadly, so do not eat any of them.

- Choose a small portion of the plant.
- Test only one part of the plant at a time.
- Break the plant into its different parts: leaves, stem, and roots.
- Smell the plant for unpleasant odors.
- Do not eat for eight hours before starting the test.
- During this period, put a piece of the plant on the inside of your elbow or wrist. Wait for 15 minutes to see if you develop a rash or burning sensation.
- During the test, do not eat anything (except the plant) and drink only pure water.
- Touch it on the outer part of your lip to test for burning or itching.
- If there is no reaction after three minutes, place it on your tongue; hold for 15 minutes.
- If there is no reaction, chew a piece thoroughly and hold it in your mouth for 15 minutes. Do not swallow.
- If there is no irritation whatsoever during this time, swallow the food.
- Wait eight hours. If you feel ill, make yourself vomit (stick two fingers down your throat) and drink plenty of water.

TEXT-DEPENDENT QUESTIONS

1. Describe the symptoms of dehydration.
2. Why shouldn't you take off clothes when you're in a survival situation in hot temperatures?
3. What are at least five ways to tell if there is water nearby?
4. How do you make a solar still?
5. List four ways to tell if you shouldn't drink the water you find in a wilderness setting.
6. Describe three different ways to get food from the wilderness.

with a spear tied to the springy shaft. This spear hits the animal when released. Warning: these traps can kill. Always approach them from behind.

You do not have to eat only animals on land. Special forces soldiers are also trained in survival fishing. There are fish in the seas, rivers, and lakes in all parts of the world, and they can be caught relatively easily. The hooks and lead weights in your survival kit are worth their weight in gold. Use the fishing methods listed here to catch fish using your line, weights, and hooks.

Still fishing

Used for catching fish on the river bed. First, weight your line, then attach a baited hook and let it settle on the bottom of the river or float. You must then sit back and be patient. Remember to pull on the line at frequent intervals to check for a bite.

RESEARCH PROJECT

This chapter mentions a few different kinds of traps and snares that can be made in the wilderness. Look up one of them online or in a book, and list each step you would need to take to build it. Draw a diagram to go along with each step. What are the dangers involved with this snare or trap?

Dry fly fishing

Different from still fishing, this method is designed to catch fish that feed on the surface of the water. Dry fly fishing is only recommended in hot weather when airborne insects are plentiful; otherwise the fish will not bite. You can improvise a line with a stick and a length of string. Cast the fly upstream and let it float down past you. Then wait for the fish to bite.

Once animal food has been caught, it should be gutted and then it can be cooked using the cooking methods we have already looked at. With plant foods, this should give you plenty to eat in the wild.

WORDS TO UNDERSTAND

vegetation: Plants.

priority: Whatever is most important.

FIRE

In the special forces, you must learn how to make fire from the natural materials around you. Fire is used not only as a heat source but also as a means of cooking food. Do not rely on matches to survive. This chapter explains how elite units make fires and keep them going.

Fire has long been one of the most important tools of human beings. From prehistoric times, humans learned how to create fire by creating friction with tools, such as saws and drills, and by producing sparks with stones such as flint. Whatever wilderness you find yourself in, a fire is always essential. A fire will provide warmth and dry clothes; it will cook food and heat drinks; it will keep wild animals at bay and ward off insects; it provides light; it can be used for signaling; and it provides a special morale booster.

In order to start and maintain a successful fire, it is vital to collect the right material and to get the balance right between the different elements of the fire, which are air, heat, and fuel.

The first material you need is tinder. This is required to get a fire started from the first sparks. Tinder can be wood shavings, thin strips of bark, sawdust, cotton fluff, bird down, dried grass, or pine straw. The next stage in fire-making is kindling. This is the material you use to really get the fire going so that you can put on larger pieces of material to burn. It includes twigs, bark, tufts of dry grass, paper, or rags soaked in fuel. Finally, there is the fuel itself. This may be wood, such as dead branches or the

One thing soldiers will never be short of in the wilderness is wood, but they must have a flint or some other fire-making equipment.

inside of trees, coal, peat (as long as it is dry enough), dry animal manure, or dry grasses twisted into bunches.

Before you actually start your fire, you have to choose somewhere to build it. Build the fire in a place where it will not be put out by a strong wind or falling snow, or where it is likely to set fire to **vegetation** or your equipment. The fire should be built on a firm base. This can be made up of stones, green wood, or solid earth. (This may involve digging down.) The fire may need to be in a hole in the ground or surrounded by rocks if wind is likely to be a problem. But there is one final point you should remember. Fires need air to burn. If you smother a fire with too many logs before it is going properly, you will snuff it out. There are a number of different kinds of fires that are suitable for different uses and areas.

Safety night fire

This type of fire is designed to burn through the night with minimal risk of falling logs. It is designed to have few air spaces, so that the flame will burn low, and two leaning logs have the effect of pushing the fire away from your shelter.

Long fire

This fire can be made either as a trench or between two parallel green logs. The logs should be thick, and may be supported by two sticks to improve the airflow.

Teepee fire

This fire is good for both cooking and heat. It is made with a slanting stick fixed into the ground over some tinder. Other sticks are then leaned on it, leaving a suitable opening on the wind side. The fire should be lit with your back to the wind.

T-fire

This is a fire kindled in a simple "T" shape carved out in the earth. It is an ideal fire for cooking on, since the main fire can be kept in the top part of the T, while cooking can be done on hot coals and embers that fall into the stem of the T.

The teepee fire is one of the best fires for air circulation.

MAKE CONNECTIONS: FIRE SAFETY

Follow these rules when making a fire to avoid getting hurt:

- Move anything that might explode well away from the fire. This includes wet stones that can blow apart if heated up.
- Do not make a fire in a shelter that has very little ventilation—the smoke will poison you.
- Clear away vegetation from around the fire—you do not want to start a forest fire.
- Make your fire in a place that you can easily escape from if the fire gets out of control.

TEXT-DEPENDENT QUESTIONS

1. List six good things fire can do for you in the wilderness.
2. What are the three elements of fire?
3. Explain the difference between tinder and kindling.
4. Describe six different kinds of fire you might build.
5. What are five safety rules you should follow whenever you build a fire?

Star fire

An economical fire that should be made with hardwood logs. The logs are arranged in a star shape and gradually pushed inward as they burn away.

Pyramid fire

Lay two logs parallel to each other, and lay a number of smaller logs across them to form a base. Lay another layer of yet smaller logs at right angles to form the next layer, and so on, until you have a small layer at the top on which to light your tinder. The fire will gradually burn downward, making it a good slow-burning fire to have during the night.

When it actually comes to lighting a fire, make sure you gather all materials in front of you before you start. Windproof matches are the easiest and most obvious way of lighting a fire—you should have a set in your survival kit. You might, however, wish to keep these for emergencies or you may have run out.

RESEARCH PROJECT

This chapter talks about using a magnifying glass to start a fire. You may have already done this—but do you know how it works? Use either the Internet or the library to look up the science behind this method of starting a fire. How does a magnifying glass work? How does something that is meant to make things look bigger also start fires? Explain what's involved. Draw a diagram to show how the process works.

If you are planning to set out on a journey, make sure you have these matches, since you will have less time when traveling to set up other means of fire lighting.

A magnifying glass can be used to light a fire. Again, you should carry a magnifying glass in your survival kit. Its advantage over matches is that it will not wear out. Angle the glass so that the sun shines through it. Then move it backward and forward until you have a single spec of hot light. Concentrate this on to some dry tinder, which should start smoking and then glow red. Blow gently to make a flame.

In your survival kit, you should have a fire-lighting piece of equipment that consists of a small saw and a small metal bar—a flint. It is easy to draw the saw across the bar to produce a strong spark. Alternatively, strike a piece of flintstone with metal for the same effect.

Fire will be a **priority** for any elite soldier making a base for the night. Of course, one of the best reasons for making a fire is for cooking. We'll look at the subject of food in the next chapter.

SHELTER

In a survival situation you must find shelter or build your own to protect you from the wind, cold, and wet. Learn from the special forces how to construct your wilderness shelter in the right place and from the proper materials.

There are several general points about shelters which you should bear in mind when you are in a survival situation in the wilderness. Of course, if you are suddenly trapped by the weather, or are injured or exhausted, almost any natural shelter will do. For example, get into a hollow in the ground and add to its height by piling up rocks around it.

There is a temptation if you are in a warm and dry climate to assume that you will need less shelter, even no shelter at all. However, remember that whatever the temperature during the day, at night it may get cold. Many warm areas can become incredibly chilly at night. In addition, a shelter can provide protection against dangers and wildlife. Snakes, for example, are attracted to body warmth and have been known to crawl into the sleeping bags of backpackers lying in the open and curl themselves up next to the sleeping person. Therefore, do not believe that you can do without shelter in the wild.

Do not build your shelter just anywhere. Make sure the ground is level; check for insects and for overhead branches that may fall on you.

Make use of tree trunks. They are a firm base to which you can lash your shelter and ensure it does not blow over in strong winds.

Choosing the right site for a shelter is very important. If you select a bad site, you will probably end up building another shelter in a better spot, and will thus waste valuable time and energy. Do not select a site in the late afternoon after a long day's walk or march. You will be tired and in no mood to make a good choice. Your decision will invariably be a bad choice and may force you into using poor materials.

The weather can also play a key part in what shelter you build and where you build it. In warm areas, build shelters in areas to take advantage of breezes, but beware of exposing a shelter to blowing sand or dust, both of which can cause injury and damage. In cold regions, choose a site that is protected from the effects of wind and drifting snow. Rain, sleet, and snow can all be **potential** hazards. Do not build a shelter where water runs, in a site that is prone to flash floods or mud slides, nor in an avalanche area.

Insects can be a problem around a camp. If you build your shelter where

MAKE CONNECTIONS: WHERE NOT TO BUILD A SHELTER

Elite forces soldiers often have to build shelters quickly when on operations behind enemy lines. They know they must avoid the following spots:

- On a hilltop exposed to wind: it will be cold and windy.
- In a valley bottom or deep hollow: they could be damp and frosty at night.
- On pieces of land that lead to water: they are often routes to animals' watering places.
- Below a tree containing a bees' or hornets' nest or dead wood. Dead wood could come crashing down on you in the next high wind.
- Under a solitary tree: it can attract lightning.

there is a breeze or steady wind, you can reduce the number of insects that will pester you. Avoid building a shelter near ponds or lakes, as it attracts mosquitoes, bees, wasps, and hornets. Do not build a shelter on or near an ant hill, unless you want lots of bites and stings!

The type of shelter you build depends on the conditions and the materials available. Remember, it is often a good idea to make a temporary shelter to give you some form of protection from the elements until you can **erect** something more permanent (particularly if it is getting dark and cold).

TEXT-DEPENDENT QUESTIONS

1. Where should you NOT build a shelter?
2. What are five things you might use to create a shelter in the wilderness?
3. What six things should a shelter provide?

If you cannot find any materials, make use of natural shelters. In open areas sit with your back to the wind and pile up equipment behind you as a windbreak.

The following are all examples of natural shelters that the survivor can use in an emergency situation:

- Brambles and boughs that sweep down to the ground or are partly broken. Add branches to make them more dense.
- Natural hollows provide protection from the wind. Use a few strong branches, covered with sticks and turf, as a roof.
- Fallen tree trunks. Scoop out a hollow on the sheltered side and cover with boughs to make a roof.
- Stones or small rocks can be used to increase the height of your hollow. To insulate against the wind, plug the gaps with turf and foliage mixed with mud.
- Caves can make excellent shelters. If it is in a cliff or mountain, increase your cave's warmth by building a windbreak over the entrance.

You can use stones, rocks, or turf cut like bricks. If you intend to light a fire in a cave, remember to light it at the back—smoke from a fire at the front of a cave will circulate against the air current and will choke you!

RESEARCH PROJECT

This chapter mentions building a windbreak as a possible way to create a shelter in the wilderness. Use the Internet or find a book on wilderness camping to find out more about how to build a windbreak. List the steps and draw a diagram for each one.

There are, of course, an almost limitless variety of shelters you can build in the wild. Use your imagination, but do not forget the basic principles. Elite soldiers are taught to build shelters that give:

• Protection from the cold.

• Protection from the snow.

• Protection from the wind.

• Protection from the damp.

• Protection from insects.

• Protection from too much sun.

WORDS TO UNDERSTAND

makeshift: A temporary substitute for something,
intended to last only for the time being.

flights: The feathers or other materials fastened to an
arrow on the opposite end from the point.

durable: Long lasting; not wearing out easily.

IMPROVISING TOOLS AND WEAPONS

The elite forces soldier is trained to make provisions including tools, weapons, and clothing, from the raw materials he or she finds in the wilderness. If carefully made, these can work better than manufactured alternatives, so practice is the key.

Being able to fashion tools from the materials you find will make your task of staying alive that much easier. It will also act as a great confidence booster. For instance, if you are stranded in the wilderness with only one knife and it breaks, it could be a disaster. However, if you are able to make an alternative, perhaps from wood or metal, your disappointment will be short-lived. In a survival situation, the number of things you can improvise is limited only by your imagination.

Club

A club has a variety of uses for the survivor. It can be used for checking snares and traps (you must not use your hands because you may get injured), killing a trapped animal, and as a weapon.

A club is extremely simple to make—so much so that if it breaks it can be replaced very easily. So whether you are in mountains or desert climates, a club will be the most useful tool you can make. All you need is a tree

Troops use a wire-cutting tool to trim wire for building shelters. If troops do not have a manufactured tool, they must improvise.

branch about two to two and a half inches (5–6 cm) in diameter and around two and a half feet (75 cm) long.

Stone tools

Although wood is probably the most plentiful natural resource for the survivor, stones and rocks are also readily available. Flint, obsidian, and quartz make good hammers. Either use them on their own or tie them to a handle.

Bone tools

The bones of any large animal can be used to make tools, so if you have snared or clubbed an animal for food, do not throw away the carcass. With improvisation, the antlers and horns of reindeer can be made into a **makeshift** spade which you can use to dig for food and water, or a hammer for building a shelter. You can even make a saw for cutting wood from discarded animal bones—a shoulder blade split in half with teeth cut along it will fit this purpose. Finally, the ribs from small animals can be sharpened into points and used as miniature spears or arrows.

Bow and arrows

The bow and arrow has been used for centuries as a hunting tool all around the world. In the United States, Native American tribes such as the Apaches, Comanches, and Sioux used them to kill buffalo and other migrating animals for hundreds of years before and after Columbus discovered the "New World" in 1492.

Above all, a bow must be springy. Yew is the best wood for this, but you

Stone and wood tools were first produced in prehistoric times. Hand axes were used in Africa and Asia about one million years ago.

nay have to use other wood if yew does not grow where you are. The bow should be about four feet (1.2 m) long. It must be two inches (5 cm) wide at he center and a half inch (1.5 cm) wide at the ends, where the wood should be notched to take the string. The arrows should be made from smooth and straight wood that is two feet (60 cm) long and a quarter inch (6 mm) wide. You should notch one end a quarter inch (6 mm) deep to fit the string of he bow. A variety of materials can be used to make **flights**, including paper, feathers, or leaves. Arrowheads can be made of tin, flint, bone, or the wood burned black. You must put a notch in the end of each arrow to fit over your bowstring.

To shoot, first place an arrow in the bowstring. Then raise the center of he bow to eye-level. Hold the bow in the center with your left hand (if you are right-handed) and rest the arrow on top of it. This arm should remain locked as you pull back the bowstring with your other hand. You must line up he target with the arrow and then release the string, making sure you do not

TEXT-DEPENDENT QUESTIONS

1. List the seven tools and weapons described in this chapter.
2. What are four different ways you might use animal bones?
3. List five things you could use as a fishhook.
4. Which tool does this chapter say is most useful? Which one is the second most useful?

snatch at it as you release. Always make sure you have several arrows, in cas you miss your target the first time.

Spears

Besides a club, a spear is the next most useful tool for killing game, and the can also be used to trap fish. A stick with a sharpened point is the simples form of spear, but this can break quite easily. A more **durable** spear will featur specially built heads. In the wilderness, you can use animal bone, flint, or ti for this purpose. They are lashed to the handle of the spear with string.

Fish hooks and lines

Improvise fish hooks from pins, a bunch of thorns, nails, bones, or wood. Yo can make a fish snare to trap large fish such as pike, which often feed alongsid weeds.

RESEARCH PROJECT

In the section of this book that describes stone tools, flint, obsidian, and quartz are listed as good stones for making makeshift hammers. Use either the Internet or a book to find out how to recognize these stones. Describe what each looks like. Explain what qualities of each stone would make it a good hammer. Print from the Internet good images of each type of stone, so that you can recognize them. If you live somewhere you can easily look for stones, try to find an actual sample of each kind of stone.

Catapult

Select a strong Y-shaped branch and a piece of elastic material. Make a pouch for the center of the elastic and thread it into position. Tie the ends of each side of the branch. Use stones or small rocks as missiles; with practice, you can become very accurate. With a sling shot, swing the sling above your head and release one end of the thong to send the ammunition in the direction of the target. When you are using a catapult against birds, use several stones at once.

The machete is an essential kit for the wilderness. "Machete" is a Spanish word, but other countries have different names for it, such as "golok," "parang," and "bolo."

WORDS TO UNDERSTAND

internationally: Having to do with countries around the world.

winched: Lifted something using a machine with a crank.

RESCUE

Though an elite forces soldier can survive for a long time in the wilderness, he or she must eventually be rescued. Here we find out the best ways of attracting rescuers to you in the wilderness.

As a survivor, it is important that you are able to give signals that a rescue team, especially an aircraft, will be able to see clearly. You must plan how you are going to be rescued and be ready to put your plan into action quickly—a rescue airplane could appear at any moment and you may not get a second chance. Unless you have a radio or flares, smoke and fire are your best ways to alert a rescue aircraft. Three fires or three columns of smoke are recognized around the world as calls for help.

If you have come down in an aircraft or are in a life raft, you may have one or more professionally made signaling tools. If you are a backpacker, you are strongly advised to equip yourself with some of the items listed below:

- Radio. Survival radios work best when you are operating in clear, open terrain.
- Hand-held flares. Day flares make a bright-colored smoke; night flares are very bright and can be seen over long distances.
- Hand-held launched flares. These are fired up into the air and can be seen from a long way away.
- Whistle. This is useful for short-range signaling.

A Canadian soldier is winched aboard a Sea King helicopter during a simulated rescue mission.

- Light signals. Flashlights or strobe lights can be seen over great distances.
- Signal mirror. A mirror flash can be visible up to a range of 100 miles (160 km) in ideal conditions. On a sunny day, mirrors, polished canteen cups, belt buckles, or other objects will reflect the sun's rays.

Smoke signals

Smoke is one of your best tools to being found. In daylight, smoke will be seen over long distances. Try to create smoke that will contrast with the environment. If you put green leaves, moss, or damp wood on a fire, you will get white smoke; rubber or oil-soaked rags on a fire will produce black smoke. At night, bright fires are better for being seen. Build a fire on a high point, or even set fire to a tree. But be careful that your fires do not get out of control.

Ground-to-air signals

Ground-to-air signals are another good method of attracting attention from the air. There are several factors you must take into account. Above all, you must try to visualize what your signal will look like when viewed by a pilot from the air. The diagram (page 54) shows the **internationally** recognized emergency signals. Learn them, or better still carry a piece of paper around with you that lists them. When laying them out, make them as large as possible, at least 40 feet (10 m) long and 10 feet (3 m) wide. At night, dig or scrape a signal in the earth, snow, or sand, then pour in gasoline and ignite it. This signal will be visible not only at night, but also during the day where the ground has been burned. You must destroy all ground-to-air symbols after rescue

MAKE CONNECTIONS:
SIGNALS USING NATURAL MATERIALS

When you are stranded in the wild, construct signals from the materials around you.

- Build brush or snow mounds that will cast shadows.
- In snow, trample down the snow to form letters or symbols and fill in the spaces with contrasting materials such as twigs or branches.
- In sand, use boulders, vegetation, or seaweed to form a symbol.
- In brush-covered areas, cut out patterns in the vegetation.
- In tundra, dig trenches or turn the soil upside down.
- In any terrain, use contrasting materials so that the symbols are visible to aircraft.

otherwise they will go on marking after you have gone. Failure to do so may result in other aircraft spotting them and attempting a rescue.

Once the rescue services know where you are, a rescue operation will be launched. On land, this will usually be in the form of a helicopter. Helicopters will make a rescue by landing or hovering. If a helicopter has to land to pick you up, do not approach it from the rear. It is a blind spot for the crew and the tail rotor is unprotected—it will kill you if it hits you. Also, be careful of being hit by the rotors if you are approaching the helicopter down a slope. Be aware of any materials on the ground that may be sucked into the rotor blades, such as a parachute or tent. Pick them up before the helicopter lands, including any leaves and twigs.

TEXT-DEPENDENT QUESTIONS

1. What is recognized around the world as a signal for help?
2. When should you use smoke as a signal? When should you use a fire?
3. List safety steps to follow if you are rescued by a helicopter.
4. Describe five ways to build signals in the wild, using materials that exist in different kinds of wilderness areas.

Try to mark the landing site with a large "H" at least 10 feet (3 m) high. However you make it, remember to make sure the materials are securely anchored to the ground so they do not fly up when the helicopter lands. If you are in sandy terrain, try to water the sand to keep dust down. In snow, try to press down the surface as much as possible. (Soft, wet snow will cling to the aircraft, and powdery snow will swirl and restrict the pilot's vision.)

If you are being **winched** aboard a hovering helicopter, let the cable touch the ground before your touch it. (All aircraft build up a lot of static electricity, and you will receive a shock if you grab it before it discharges into the ground.) Fit yourself into the harness and then give the "thumbs up" sign. Do not make any further signals, especially raising your arms—you could slip out of the harness.

When you get to the cabin door, let the winchman do everything and obey everything he says. When you are out of the winch, you will be told to sit down and shown where to sit. Go immediately to this place to be fastened into the seat. Remember to obey the aircrew at all times. Be careful when you leave

RESEARCH PROJECT

The chapter shows you eight ground-to-air symbols, but there are many more. Use a book or the Internet to find them. Make a chart with 25 different symbols, drawing each symbol yourself and then explaining what it means.

the helicopter after it has touched down; wait for the rotors to stop turning—obey crew members at all times.

Once you are rescued, your survival situation is at an end. Helicopter and other rescue crews are called out to thousands of rescues each year. Most could have been avoided if the people had approached their outdoor adventure sensibly. Remember, you should be trained in survival, but you should never have to use your skills!

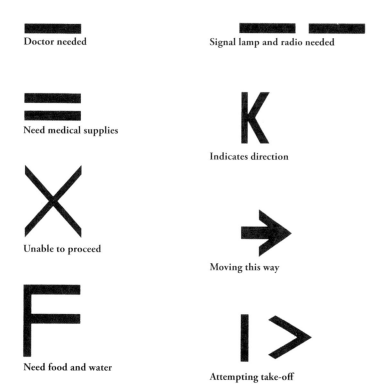

Doctor needed

Signal lamp and radio needed

Need medical supplies

Indicates direction

Unable to proceed

Moving this way

Need food and water

Attempting take-off

Some of the internationally recognized ground-to-air signals used when trying to attract rescue.

WORDS TO UNDERSTAND

hypothermia: A dangerous condition where body temperature falls too low.

frostbite: Injury to the body from extreme cold. The nose, fingers, and toes are the body parts most likely to be frostbitten.

aggressive: Ready to be violent.

carnivorous: Meat-eating.

prevalent: Common.

DANGERS

If you get ill in the wilderness, your chances of survival are not good. If you act fast, and use elite forces training, the chances of coming through are much, much better.

The wilderness regions are full of dangers that the elite soldier must face with courage and skill. The main dangers are cold and heat. You must get out of the elements straight away and build a shelter. Otherwise you could find yourself falling victim to a wide range of illnesses, including dehydration, **hypothermia**, **frostbite**, sunburn, and trench foot.

Trench foot is an injury many elite soldiers had to fight in various wars. It is caused by the feet being constantly cold and wet. In the early stages, feet and toes appear pale and feel numb, cold, and stiff. Walking is difficult and the feet swell and become painful. You must be alert to prevent trench foot: it can lead to amputation. To prevent trench foot, make sure you clean and dry your socks and boots regularly, and dry your feet as quickly as possible if they get wet. If wearing wet boots and socks, exercise your feet continually by wriggling your toes and bending your ankles. When treating trench foot, handle the feet very gently. Do not rub or massage them. Clean carefully with soap and water, dry, and then raise them up. Do not walk if you have trench foot.

In the wilderness, you are also vulnerable to various illnesses carried by insects. You must try to prevent these illnesses through keeping clean. Try not to get cuts and scratches: in the wilderness, they can become infected very

A soldier from the Australian SAS regiment diffuses a mine in the Australian outback during Exercise "Tandem Thrust."

easily. Clean all cooking and eating utensils, dispose of garbage and human wastes, and protect food and utensils from flies. Do not expose your skin to the weather or to flies. Try to wash your feet and body daily. Change your socks regularly. You must check yourself for signs of any injury, and cover up any wounds with an adhesive bandage.

Animals are another danger. Bears are present in the northern forests and wastes. Steer clear of them: they are powerful and dangerous and can be killers, particularly when they have young. Bears are powerful and tireless creatures that can pursue you for miles. Do not leave food scattered around your camp, as this will attract bears to you. Under no circumstances try to feed bears. Wild pigs have an **aggressive** nature and should be treated with caution. Some small pigs travel in groups of between 5 and 15, and in these numbers they can easily overcome a human. It is best to try to kill them at a distance with a spear. Do not try to tackle them yourself: their tusks can inflict severe injuries to your legs.

Even more than these larger animals, insects perhaps create the greater problems in wilderness survival. There are several types of dangerous or unpleasant insects and and other small creatures that you will need to avoid in the wilderness.

Ants

Red ants live in pinewoods where they build nests as giant mounds. They live in groups of thousands and will bite viciously if they are disturbed.

Centipedes

There are some 3,000 species of centipede. They are **carnivorous** and feed mainly on a diet of worms. Mostly they are harmless, but some of the larger varieties will bite.

RESEARCH PROJECT

There are certain plants that elite soldiers know not to eat in the wilderness. Find a good plant book or go online and learn to identify all the plants listed below. Make a chart using the material provided here. Include in the chart a drawing of each plant or print an image from the Internet. Then look up which ones grow in your area and put a star next to these plants on your chart. Are there any other poisonous plants in the region where you live? You can find out using books and the Internet. If there are, add them to your list, describing their dangers and including an image of each.

PLANT	EFFECT
Poison sumac	Irritates skin
Poison ivy	Skin irritation and rash
Thorn-apple	Can kill if swallowed
Foxglove	Attacks the heart and can lead to death if eaten
Hemlock	Will create severe illness if eaten
Water hemlock/Cowbane	Lethal even if only one mouthful is ingested
Deadly nightshade	All parts of the plant are potentially lethal

TEXT-DEPENDENT QUESTIONS

1. What are the two biggest dangers in the wilderness?
2. What is trench foot?
3. List seven insects and other creatures that can be dangerous in the wilderness.
4. What are five ways to protect yourself from insects?

Hornets, bees, and wasps

All of these insects give painful stings, which in some cases can be fatal. It is important that you check for nesting sites before building a shelter. In particular, wasps attack moving targets, so either remain still or hide in dense undergrowth where it will be difficult for the swarm to find you.

Scorpions

These are common in hot regions all over the world. Scorpions are characterized by two crablike pincers either side of the head, which are used to trap prey, and a poisonous spike in the tail.

Black widow spider

This is dangerously poisonous. Its bite can cause the human heart to stop in some cases.

Funnel-web spider

This is deadly poisonous. Found in Australia, it is medium to large and black with long legs.

Ticks

Common in many areas of the world, ticks feed on blood. They have very powerful jaws for such small insects, which become embedded in the skin. To remove, use fine-tipped tweezers and grasp the tick as close to the skin's surface as possible. Pull upward with steady, even pressure. Never jerk or twist the tick; this can cause the mouth-parts to break off and remain in the skin. After removing the tick, thoroughly clean the area and your hands with rubbing alcohol. Never use heat or alcohol in an attempt to remove the tick.

With all insects, the soldiers of the special forces follow a set of rules that protect them from getting bitten. Remember the following tips when surviving in the wilderness: use insect repellent on exposed areas of skin; always wear clothing, especially at night when insects are more **prevalent**; wear gloves and a head net; camp well away from swamps; sleep under mosquito netting if you have it, or smear mud on your face to keep the insects away.

SERIES GLOSSARY
OF KEY TERMS

camouflage: Something that makes it hard to distinguish someone or something from the terrain or landscape around them.

casualty: A person who is killed or injured in a war or accident.

covert: Done in secret.

dehydrated: When you don't have enough water in your body for it to function properly. Alternatively, dehydrated food is food that has had all the water removed so that it won't go bad.

dislocation: When a joint is separated; when a bone comes out of its socket.

edible: Able to be eaten.

exposure: A health condition that results from bad weather around you. For example, when you get hypothermia or frostbite from cold weather, these are the results of exposure.

flares: A device that burns brightly, and can be used to signal for help. They can only be used once.

hygiene: The techniques and practices involved with keeping yourself clean and healthy.

improvised: Used whatever was available to make or create something. When you don't have professionally made equipment, you can make improvised equipment from the materials naturally found around you.

insulation: Something that keeps you warm and protects you from the cold.

kit: All of the clothing and equipment carried by a soldier.

layering: A technique of dressing for the wilderness that involves wearing many layers of clothing. If you become too warm or too cold, it is easy to remove or add a layer.

marine: Having to do with the ocean.

morale: Confidence, enthusiasm, and discipline at any given time. When morale is high, you are emotionally prepared to do something difficult. When morale is low, you might be angry, scared, or anxious.

purification: The process of making water clean and safe enough to drink.

terrain: The physical features of a stretch of land. Hard or rough terrain might be mountains or thick forests, and easy terrain would be an open field.

windbreak: Something that you use to block the wind from hitting you. If you camp somewhere exposed to the wind, it will be very difficult to stay warm.

FURTHER READING

Davenport, Gregory J. *Wilderness Survival: 2nd Edition.* Mechanicsburg, Penn.: Stackpole Books, 2006.

Isaac, Jeffrey. *The Outward Bound Wilderness First-Aid Handbook, Revised and Updated.* Guilford, Conn.: Falcon Publishing, 2008.

McPherson, John and McPherson, Geri. *Ultimate Guide to Wilderness Living: Surviving with Nothing But Your Bare Hands and What You Find in the Woods.* Berkeley, Calif.: Ulysses Press, 2008.

Montgomery, David. *Mountainman Crafts and Skills: A Fully Illustrated Guide to Wilderness Living and Survival (2nd Edition).* New York: Lyons Press, 2008

Stillwell, Alexander. *The Encyclopedia of Survival Techniques.* New York: The Lyons Press, 2008.

Wiseman, John. *The SAS Survival Handbook.* New York: HarperCollins, 2009.

ABOUT THE AUTHOR

Dr. Chris McNab has written and edited numerous books on military history and elite forces survival. His publications to date include *German Paratroopers of World War II, The Illustrated History of the Vietnam War, First Aid Survival Manual,* and *Special Forces Endurance Techniques,* as well as many articles and features in other works. Forthcoming publications include books on the SAS, while Chris's wider research interests lie in literature and ancient history. Chris lives in South Wales, U.K.

INDEX

DATE DUE

LAKE PARK HIGH SCHOOL
ROSELLE, IL 60172